Worlds Gr

This book Is to be returned on or before
the last date stamped below.

10 2 NOV 2005 **MOBILE** 7 8 APR 2008

2 3 NOV 2005 2 0 JAN 2009

7 5 DEC 2005 0 6 DEC 2006 1 1 DEC 2009

2 4 MAR 2006 2 0 DEC 2006 2 1 MAY 2010

1 5 MAY 2006 0 5 FEB 2007 0 9 FEB 2011

7 6 JUN 2006 0 9 APR 2007

10 2 OCT 2006 1 8 JUN 2007

2 5 OCT 2006 1 8 DEC 2007

2 2 NOV 2006 0 8 FEB 2008

ACKNOWLEDGMENTS

I wish to thank the following people for sharing practical jokes which are included in this book: Liz Abramson, David Albert, Thomas Beddall, Lenny-Bob Cohen, Eddie Costikyan, Jill and Gerry Finkelstein, Bob Goudie, Clem and Debby Herschel, Jane Loeffler, Petar Mrkic, Noemi Millman, Joan Nyman, Jim Oliensis (for Marc Antony's fish), the Olmstead family, Sascha Paladino, Catherine Ross, Jonathan Schulz, Benjamin Smith, Emlen Smith, Pamela Smith, Robert Smith, Robert S. Smith, Rosemary Smith, and Eric and Jackie Yecies.

I am also grateful to my family for their general good humor while being the guinea pigs on which these practical jokes were tested.

Edited by Claire Bazinet

Library of Congress Cataloging-in-Publication Data Available

10 9 8 7 6 5 4 3 2 1

Published by Sterling Publishing Co., Inc.
387 Park Avenue South, New York, NY 10016
© 2004 by Dian G. Smith
Distributed in Canada by Sterling Publishing
c/o Canadian Manda Group, One Atlantic Avenue, Suite 105
Toronto, Ontario, Canada M6K 3E7
Distributed in Great Britain and Europe by Chris Lloyd at Orca Book
Services, Stanley House, Fleets Lane, Poole BH15 3AJ, England

Manufactured in the United States of America
Sterling ISBN 1-4027-1020-8

Contents

Preface

Once a year, just before April Fools' Day, store shelves begin to pile high with the same tired old gags: hand buzzers, snapping gum, pepper candy, rubber eggs, plastic ink stains. Some are pretty good; some are pretty bad. All of them you have seen before and will see again and again.

But what about the rest of the year? What if you're the kind of joker who gets an irresistible itch to liven things up a bit on one of the 364 days that is not April 1st? And what if you have a yen to do something clever and outrageous, not just plunk down your money and tear open a package?

That's why you need this book. Here is a supply of tricks for all seasons, all days, all hours, and all types of victims. Some have to be planned carefully in advance. For others, you will need only a few minutes alone to do your dirty work. Most require few supplies, and some just a straight face or a gullible victim. Some are big jokes for people with great senses of humor (mostly kids). Some are smaller—for parents, camp counselors, and the right sort of teachers.

With this book in hand, you'll join a long, distinguished line of practical jokers. Over 2,000 years ago, for example, Marc Antony tried to impress Cleopatra with his fishing skill by sending a diver underwater to attach big fish to his line. The sly queen saw through his trick and decided to play one of her own. Her diver, arriving first, hooked on a salted herring for Antony to pull in instead.

Much more recently, on an April Fools' Day, Penn Jillette of the weird magic-and-comedy act Penn & Teller placed an ad in a magazine offering to sell a super-high-tech computer system worth $20,000 for a mere $1,278.43. The many bargain-hunters who eagerly dialed the phone number printed in the ad heard this recorded message: "You, my credulous friend, have been had...." And on that same mystical day, about ten miles from Los Angeles International Airport, a couple of big-thinking jokers mounted a huge sign on the roof of a racetrack for incoming air travelers to see. It read: "Welcome to CHICAGO."

Is there a secret to being a successful practical joker? Yes. Always aim for the funny bone. Practical jokes that destroy property or hurt feelings are not funny. They are mean. All the jokes in this book are meant to be reversible. Once the joke is over, you—the joker—should be willing to undo any temporary disorder or damage it caused.

Remember, though, that hurt feelings are not so easily undone, so choose your victims carefully. A practical joke is not funny if, in the end, your victim feels like crying, not laughing. Remember, too, that one good joke deserves another. Be a good sport when the tables are turned and the joke is on you.

Dian G. Smith

1. Good Enough to Eat

Are you in the mood for cooking up some mischief? If so, here is the place to start. Wait until the kitchen is empty, then sneak in with this book. Listed above each practical joke are the ingredients you will need. Most of them you will find right on the shelves in front of you.

Pass the Salt 1

You'll need:
- **salt**
- **sugar**

Substituting salt for sugar is an old but brilliant trick—quick, simple, and effective. The white crystals look identical to the casual eye, but their flavors couldn't be more different. The key element here is surprise. Don't play this trick on April Fools' Day. Suspicions are high then and a cautious tasting finger is likely to precede any spoon into the sugar bowl. On any other day of the year, however, it's nearly foolproof—assuring you the evil pleasure of watching your victim react to a mouthful of salty cereal or sugar-sweetened meat.

Consider also a twist on the standard salt-in-the-sugar-bowl gag. Even though sugar crystals are larger, they will sift convincingly through the holes of most salt shakers. For a grander (and more daring) effect, fill an empty salt carton with sugar and the sugar canister with salt.

Pass the Salt II

You'll need:
- **salt**
- **pepper**

Also a classic, the trick here is to switch salt and pepper. This is particularly effective when the shakers are clear glass. Fill each to just above the level where the top screws on, hiding the uppermost contents. Press a piece of napkin or paper towel down inside the shaker to protect the salt or pepper. Then pour a small amount of the "other" seasoning on top of the napkin.

This technique offers two advantages to an out-and-out switch, which would be impossible with clear shakers in any case. First, surprise: It is a shock to see pepper pour out of a glass container that you can clearly see holds salt! Second, reversibility: Once the small amount of salt and pepper on top is poured out and you remove the napkin, order is restored.

Milk Mix-up

You'll need:
- **buttermilk**

Buttermilk is the ideal milk substitute. It fools the eye but not the tongue. Made from sweet milk with most of the butterfat removed, it is extremely sour. It is also, actually, good for you—if you can manage to develop a taste for it.

The simplest way to serve buttermilk to the unsuspecting is to pour it into glasses in advance. It comes in a carton like milk does, but someone may spot the fraud. Pour yourself a glass, too (of regular milk), and drink heartily to set the mood. If, instead, you use a pitcher for the buttermilk, you'll have the pleasure of watching your intended victims pour it into their coffee and onto their cereal themselves.

Better yet, retrieve an empty and discarded milk carton a few days beforehand. Wash it thoroughly and let it dry. Then, one night just before bedtime, transfer the buttermilk into the milk carton. It will be worth waking up early the next morning to watch the fun.

Breakfast of Champions I

You'll need:
- **2 boxes of breakfast cereal**

The best time to play practical jokes is early in the morning. Your victims are usually still too sleepy to notice telltale details. So try this simple breakfast gag. Choose two boxes of different cereals that are the same size. Remove the inner bags from each and return them to the wrong boxes. Sit down to breakfast with your family. How long will it take them to figure out the switch—and who did it?

Breakfast of Champions II

You'll need:
- **cereal box**
- **grapes, popped popcorn, potato chips, or crayons**

This version of the trick is more dramatic but also requires more advance planning. Save an empty box of your family's favorite cereal. Fill it with grapes, popped popcorn, potato chips, or crayons. These will not raise suspicion by making the box too light or heavy. Enjoy the surprise of your victims when the unexpected contents come pouring out.

Have a Sip

You'll need:
  • **drinking straw**

Did you ever try to suck through a paper straw that has collapsed, or drink a very thick shake using a thin straw? You pulled and pulled but nothing happened, right? Your victim will have a similar experience, but for no clear reason. The trick is to make a small hole (about ¼-inch) in the straw a few inches down from the top. (Face it away from your victim when you hand it to him.) Because air will enter the straw through this hole, it will be impossible for the drinker to create the vacuum needed in the straw to draw the liquid upward. Of course, if you "test out" the straw when your victim complains (covering the hole with your finger), you won't have any trouble.

Color Me Tasteless I

You'll need:
- **food coloring**
- **empty juice container**
- **grapefruit juice, seltzer, or club soda**

Food colorings are a basic tool in any bag of tricks, offering endless possibilities for deception. The simplest of these is replacing juice with water. Wait until a bottle of cranberry, grape, or apple juice is almost empty. Save the last small cupful for matching color. Wash out the bottle and fill it with water. Mix in the food dyes (red and blue for grape; red for cranberry; yellow for apple) until you've matched your sample. For orange juice, which is often pulpy, use grapefruit juice as your base and add yellow. For orange, grape, or cherry soda, add coloring to a clear, carbonated beverage, such as club soda or seltzer.

Color Me Tasteless II

You'll need:
- **food coloring**
- **unflavored gelatin**

Feeling a bit more ambitious? Volunteer to make a Jell-O® dessert, then use a package of unflavored gelatin and add water you've colored yellow, red, orange, or green. Serve yourself, too, and smile…as if there's nothing at all wrong.

Hard as an Egg

You'll need:
- 1 egg

Try this if you don't mind eating egg salad for supper. The trick is to replace a raw egg in your refrigerator with a hard-boiled one. When someone tries to crack it for a recipe... surprise!

To hardboil an egg, you'll need the help of someone who is allowed to use the stove. Place the egg in a small pot on the burner and cover it with cold water. Turn the heat to medium. When the water is just about to boil, turn the heat down and let it simmer (the point at which tiny bubbles form around the edges of the pot) for about 20 minutes. Turn off the heat and pour cold water into the pot. When the water has finally cooled down the egg, which stays hot much longer, remove the egg.

By the way, if you forget which is the hardboiled egg, lay the eggs on their sides and spin them. The spin of the hard-boiled egg will be faster and less wobbly.

Truth in Labeling

You'll need:
- **2 labeled food cans
  of the same size**

This idea comes from a man who lived through the Great Depression in the United States during the 1930s. He remembers his mother bringing home canned goods she bought cheap at the market because they had lost their labels. He also remembers eating some very odd meals.

You can surprise your unsuspecting family, too, by switching the labels on same-size cans in your cupboard (baked beans and peeled tomatoes, for example; or peas and cream of mushroom soup). The labels usually are attached by only a few spots of glue. Pry them off carefully, trying not to tear them, then glue them onto the other cans.

Don't forget along the way which is which! You will add to your victim's good humor without losing any of the fun if, after a good laugh, you can replace the labels on the proper cans or mark them correctly.

Say "Cheese"

You'll need:
- **bar of soap**

Do you know someone who snacks on cheese and crackers or eats cheese sandwiches for lunch? If so, here is a trick recipe for you. Replace the cheese slices with slices of soap. Cut them off a bar of soap with a cheese slicer or butter knife (not a sharp knife). If you don't have soap the color of American cheese, use a white soap and say it is mozzarella or white cheddar. (If the soap lunch is at school, make peace by having a replacement snack handy.)

P.B. and Worms

You'll need:
- **sandwich (peanut butter & jelly, or other)**
- **cooked spaghetti**

Pack a specially-made, squirmy worms sandwich for school lunch and you're sure to get a big reaction. The worms aren't real, of course. Just take your usual sandwich, maybe peanut butter and your favorite jelly, and add some strands of cooked spaghetti in between. Fix them to hang partially out the sides to wiggle and squirm as you eat. The spaghetti won't affect the taste, but it's sure to ruin everyone else's appetite.

Don't care for sandwiches? Adding a few spaghetti "worms" to a pudding snack—like dark chocolate—should start some stomachs churning. Offer to share, of course.

Don't Cry over Spilt Milk

You'll need:
- **half-empty drink carton**

What's more embarrassing than spilling milk? Having no idea how it happened. For this trick you need a partly empty drink carton—the paper kind with the peaked top. On the spout side, make a small hole with a pencil or pen about an inch below the crease. If you hand the carton to a victim, do it with the hole facing away. But if it's just picked up, don't worry. They're still unlikely to spot the hole. Then, as the carton is tipped to pour the milk, the liquid will come out the spill hole before reaching the spout.

After having a good laugh and helping to clean up the mess, repair the damage by taping up the hole (wrap some tape around the whole carton to secure it well).

Dribble Cup

You'll need:
- **paper cup**

For this trick, you don't need a whole carton of milk. A dribble cup is a "special" cup, with a hole so liquid will dribble out and down a victim's chin. Just punch a small hole an inch or so below the rim. The trick is to keep your victim from noticing the rigged cup. Set two filled cups out on a low table, so that the one with the hole is facing your victim. Take your cup and begin to drink, and he or she will automatically follow.

Note: Don't play this trick on someone who is wearing silk (which stains easily) or dressed for a fancy party. They are certain not to laugh—and you had better not either!

Surprise Inside

You'll need:
- **plain chocolate bar**
- **round sweet pickle slices**

Place an unwrapped chocolate bar on a plate and melt it in the hot summer sun or near a radiator in winter. Dry some pickle slices with paper towels. When the chocolate is completely melted, dip the pickle slices in it one at a time, coating all the sides and edges. Place them on a plate and refrigerate until the chocolate has hardened. Use a spatula to loosen any that have stuck to the plate, and you'll have delicious-looking homemade "sweets" to offer for dessert.

Designer Ice Cubes

You'll need:
- **ice cube tray**
- **food colorings or ketchup**

There are several ways to use ice cubes to sabotage drinks. The simplest trick is to color water with food dyes before freezing it in the ice cube tray. But some tricksters prefer to create a more subtle effect. Here's one: Fill an ice cube tray with tap water, then add one or two drops of ketchup to each section, and freeze.

These red-eyed (or bloody!) cubes work best in water or a light-colored drink, such as lemonade. Be sure to stay cool yourself while your victims try to figure out what is wrong with their drinks.

Finger-licking Good

You'll need:
- **1 can foamy shaving cream**

Shaving cream is a perfect look-alike for whipped cream, but do you really want to face the consequences of destroying a favorite whipped cream-covered dessert or a mouth-watering hot-fudge sundae complete with sprinkles? (You had better be a fast runner!)

For a milder trick, still good for a lot of laughs, fill a small mixing bowl with shaving cream, cover it with plastic wrap, and put it in the refrigerator. Then wait for your unwary victims to stick in a finger to get a taste.

No sneak thieves? Remove most of the shaving cream, leaving just a little around the sides of the bowl, and leave it out. It will look like someone just made whipped cream and didn't clean up. Still no takers? Looks like you'll have to be generous and offer it to a brother or sister.

Get the Scoop

You'll need:
- **cream cheese**

Form cream cheese into a ball the size of a scoop of ice cream and put it in the freezer. Then offer, "Does anyone want ice cream?" Take and fill the orders, choosing your victim from among those who ask for vanilla. Be generous with the toppings, especially the chocolate sauce.

Doggone Good

You'll need:
- **frosting or whipped cream**
- **dog biscuits**

Buy or make some frosting or whipped cream and smooth it over dog biscuits. (The bone-shaped ones tend to give the trick away, but these pet treats come in all sorts of shapes and sizes these days.) Your friends might make faces after a taste and refuse to eat them. If you serve these delicacies to adults, however, they may be too polite to complain.

Note: Dog biscuits generally have no ingredients that may be harmful to humans but, just to be sure, check the package for any such warnings.

Oreo-oh-oh

You'll need:
- **chocolate sandwich cookies**
- **cream cheese**

Offer to prepare a plate of assorted cookies for a snack or dessert, including four chocolate sandwich cookies. Choose three of these as trick cookies and place the fourth in a spot on the plate where you can easily find it. Carefully open the other three sandwich cookies and scrape off the white filling inside. Replace the filling with an equal amount of cream cheese, nicely rounded off so it looks just like it did before, and close the cookie. As you serve dessert, take the regular cookie for yourself, commenting on how delicious it is.

Since cream cheese needs to be refrigerated, don't let the trick cookies sit out for more than an hour—although this usually is not a problem with cookies.

Oh, Nuts!

You'll need:
- **unshelled nuts**
- **glue**
- **any filling**

Does your family ever serve unshelled nuts? If so, here is a slick trick to pull on them. When no one is looking, sneak away with the nutcracker and a nut or two that look easy to open. (Walnuts and roasted peanuts are good possibilities.) Carefully break the shell open (into halves or as few pieces as possible). Remove the nut meat and replace it with something you usually don't find in a nutshell.

Your choice of "filling" may be a note saying "April Fool!" or "Sorry, we got here first, [signed] Alvin and the Chipmunks," a fortune cookie note, or something aimed at a special victim, like, "Your tuba playing drives me nuts!"

Or you might put one of these small items inside:

a tightly wound metal or paper spring

a lump of clay with a happy face in it

tiny origami

a ring or small earrings (for your favorite girl)

peanuts (in a walnut shell!)

a smooth rock with eyes painted on it

Valentine heart candy

a shiny coin

peanut butter

or nothing at all!

Then put the halves or pieces back together with white glue and return the nutcracker and the dummy nut to the top of the bowl. If there are lots of nuts in the bowl, or you simply can't wait, confiscate some of the nuts or offer a few, including the doctored nut, to your intended target.

2. The Switch Is On

With these jokes, there is the delicious added element of disbelief—that Alice-in-Wonderland feeling that things are not what they seem. For Alice, what is clearly a baby is surely a pig. For your victim, what is clearly a physics textbook is instead an Italian cookbook.

Old News

You'll need:
- **copy of old newspaper or magazine**

This trick works best on people (usually moms, dads, or friendly neighbors) who have their newspapers delivered in the morning. Retrieve a discarded newspaper, fold it crisply back into shape, and save it for several weeks. On D-for-Delivery Day (which should be the same day of the week), get up early and substitute this paper for the one at the door.

For a slightly more subtle variation, just wrap the outer sheet, front and back, from the new paper around the inner section of the old paper. How long will it be until someone notices that the "news" inside is actually old?

If papers aren't delivered, you can play this trick with a magazine that arrives in the mail. In this case, remove the cover from an old copy of the magazine. Wait several weeks or months. When a new issue arrives, carefully remove the cover and attach it to the old magazine.

Misprints

You'll need:
- **newspaper**

Adults rely on their morning newspaper, and many of them have firm habits about when, where, and how they read it. This trick should shake them up.

Get to the paper as soon as it is delivered. Open it flat and remove the top sheet. Turn it over to begin a pile. Next, turn the second sheet upside down and place it on the first. Make the page after that right side up, the next upside down…and so on. When you are done, turn the whole pile over and fold the paper to look as it did when it came.

A variation of this is to simply mix up the sheets. Since they will all be facing the same way, it may take your victim even longer to figure out what has happened—and go looking for the culprit.

Two Left Feet

You'll need:
- **men's shoes**

This trick works best with men's shoes, which tend to look more alike than women's. Create new pairs of two lefts and two rights of similar looking shoes, such as black or brown loafers. This works best on a weekday morning when your dad or older brother is groggily getting dressed for work or school.

Don't Judge a Book by Its Cover

You'll need:
- **2 hardcover books of the same size**

This trick is best done at home because you are more likely to know the habits of people with whom you live. Notice the books that your parents or siblings carry from home to school or work, or keep on a night table for bedtime reading. Choose one that has a jacket and measure its length, width, and thickness. Now, find a totally different book with the same measurements: an Italian pasta cookbook in place of a hefty biology book, for example; or a Latin dictionary for a novel. Slip the new book into the cover of the old and return it to its original location.

To take credit for your mischief, slip a bookmark onto page 13 (an appropriate place) and write whatever message you wish. Be prepared to return the purloined book immediately on demand—and for any possible revenge.

Misfits

You'll need:
- **identical clothes in different sizes**

This trick works best in families with lots of males, since boys' clothing is often modeled after their Dads'. But don't give up if your family is heavy on females. Many a mother, rushed or still groggy with sleep, has struggled to squeeze herself into her 8-year-old's bikini underpants before realizing her mistake. You get the idea?

One day, just after the clean laundry has been put away, quietly and neatly exchange Dad's underwear (or plain-color socks, shirts, turtlenecks, or jeans) with one of the boys' in the family who is smaller but not too obviously smaller.

If you have a lot of siblings, you could skip Mom and Dad altogether and play this switch on some of your brothers or sisters. The beauty of it is that you can take in two victims with a single prank, and there are more suspects to go around.

Color Blind

You'll need:
- **brown, blue, black socks**

In the early morning light it is very hard to tell one color from another, especially if someone is still only half-awake anyway—someone like your father, perhaps. Socks that are black, blue, and brown will all look alike to him. Besides, if two socks are rolled together as a pair, it is natural to assume that they are a pair. He may not even bother to look.

Choose a time when you can be alone for about fifteen minutes in your parents' bedroom. Unroll all your father's socks and make new pairs of the blues, browns, and blacks. Be careful as you mismatch colors to match the sock lengths. Sometime later in the day, in the bright sunlight, your father will look down and be quite surprised.

Mix and Match

You'll need:
- **pair of similar looking suits**

Here's a trick to play on someone who wears suits to work every day that look pretty much the same (probably your father). Suit pants, jackets, and sometimes vests are usually hung together in a closet on the same hanger. They're also put on early in the morning when the wearer is not at his peak of alertness. Your job is to find two suits that look very similar—the same color but slightly different fabrics or designs. Then just switch the pants of one for the pants of the other. Be patient. It may be several days before the suit you've "altered" is chosen to be worn, and it may be several hours before the trick is discovered. Don't give it away by an overeager interest in your victim's wardrobe.

Home Runs

You'll need:
- **6 pair of stockings with runs**

Women who wear stockings are sometimes tormented by runs. When in a hurry, they will quickly pull on a pair of pantyhose, discover a run, tear the stockings off, toss them aside, and reach frantically for a new pair. If that sounds like your mom or older sister, here's your chance to drive her crazy. Retrieve those stockings from the wastebasket and wash and save them until you have about six pair. Then secretly remove good stockings from the drawer and replace them with the runny duds—folded or rolled the usual way. Wait for the screams.

All-Natural Shampoo

You'll need:
- **empty shampoo bottle**
- **ketchup, mayonnaise, syrup, etc.**

Natural shampoos are the rage these days, many containing the full array of fruits and vegetables from apples to zucchini. So why not cook up a surprise version from items in your own kitchen? A sister, if you have one, will usually have the most dramatic reaction to this trick, although any teenager these days will probably raise a satisfactory fuss.

Start by retrieving an empty shampoo bottle from the wastebasket. Wash and dry it, then look in the food cupboard. Mayonnaise, catsup, or pancake syrup are all good choices, but feel free to use your imagination. Fill the bottle to about one-third of its volume. Wait until your victim's new bottle of shampoo is at that level, then make the switch.

Key to Unhappiness 1

You'll need:
- **2 similar-looking keys**

Have you ever had your key stick in a lock? You tug and twist, turn the key upside down, and tug and twist again. Finally, for some unknown reason, everything clicks. That is, of course, because you do have the right key. In this trick, your victim does not.

Start saving keys. Look for ones similar to your house, garage, or car keys, your sister's or brother's bike lock or locker key, or the keys your parents use to get into their places of work. When you find one, put it on your victim's key chain and remove its match. Leave the original key where it's easy to find, or return it—before someone decides to take the lock apart!

Warning: Keys look very much alike and some are not easily replaceable. Small scratch marks on found fakes will help you keep track of which is which!

Key to Unhappiness II

You'll need:
- **several hotel key cards**

Many motels and hotels these days use key cards rather than keys. They slip into slots in room doors and set off a mechanism to open them. These cards usually come in envelopes with the room number, but are not themselves marked.

When your family stays at a hotel and uses more than one room, it's possible to cause havoc by switching the cards —the more rooms, the more havoc. Another option, if you travel often, is to save key cards from whatever hotels you visit (they deactivate when you check out), and slip these into the new envelopes as replacements. Your unsuspecting victim is unlikely to take the time to check and read the name of the hotel on the card (if there is one) until he has already pounded and kicked the door in frustration.

3. School Scams

Do these at your own risk. Keep in mind that if you haven't turned in your math homework in a week, that teacher is not likely to just laugh your joke away.

As for kids, don't expect the goodie-goodie in the first row to enjoy having a lesson disrupted, especially if he or she is the target of your joke.

Crash!

You'll need:
- **clear nylon thread**

Here is a trick to play on a teacher with a sense of humor or on a parent who has a desk at home. Push the chair tightly against the desk. Tie one end of a long piece of clear nylon thread or fishing leader to the back of the chair. Tie the other end tightly to an object at the far end on top of the desk. Make sure there is nothing breakable or spillable in its path. When your teacher or parent pulls the chair out, an avalanche of objects on the desk will come tumbling down.

If your intended victim is a neat freak, with a perfectly clean desk, don't despair. Tie the thread instead to the front legs of the chair and the back legs of the desk.

Chalkboard Mischief

You'll need:
- **double-sided chalkboard or pull-down chart**

This trick works best on the double-sided chalkboards some teachers use. They either flip over or revolve on wheels. Sneak into your classroom early or stay late and write a message or draw a picture on the back side of the board. Here are some: "Greetings from Guess Who?" "Help! I'm trapped inside this chalkboard!" "Class will be dismissed 30 minutes early today [signed by the principal]." "Ms. X [the teacher] loves Mr. Y." Be careful to choose something that will get a laugh, not send you to detention for a month. If there's no chalkboard in your classroom, maybe you can attach your message to a pull-down map or chart with masking tape. Be careful, though, not to harm surfaces doing this. Never use tape on movie screens, which are fragile and easily damaged.

Post It

You'll need:
- **paper and tape, or Post-It®**

If you are looking for something to brighten the school day, try this simple trick: stick a message to someone's back (a kid or, depending on what you write, a teacher). There are an infinite number of possible messages, but the best ones are tailored to the victim. Here are a few old stand-bys:

Write your message on a slip of paper and add a strip of

TICKLE ME	SNARL AT ME
MARRY ME	HOWL AT ME
BLOW ME A KISS	SNEEZE AS YOU GO BY
HUG ME	LAUGH AS YOU GO BY
SAY "HAPPY BIRTHDAY"	SLAP ME FIVE
SAY "HEE-HAW"	or the classic,
BEEP AT ME	I'M AN APRIL FOOL

tape across the top, or use ready-made stick-on notes (such as Post-It®) with glue already at the top. Hiding the paper behind you, draw your victim over. Then, friendly-like, casually reach your arm around and lightly pat the message into place on his or her back.

Pass It On

You'll need:
- **note paper**

Do you ever pass notes in class? If so, try this one and watch what happens:

SMILE IF YOU'RE NOT WEARING UNDERWEAR

Almost any kid who reads this will smile automatically—and then feel like an absolute jerk. Use your creativity to come up with other embarrassing phrases to put after the "smile if."

Be sure to write PASS IT ON at the end of the note, so all your victims can also share in the fun.

Heavy Course Load

You'll need:
- **heavy rocks**

Kids are always complaining to their parents and teachers that they get too much homework, and the weight of their backpacks is solid evidence of that. So here is a way to support your siblings or friends...and get a good laugh. When they're not looking, bury a heavy rock or two underneath the textbooks in each pack. Add a rock or two to your own backpack to disguise the deed, or to bolster your own claim.

A Disappearing Act

You'll need:
- **class of students**

If you have the type of teacher (often the math teacher) who turns away for long periods of time to write on the chalkboard, it's possible to give him or her a pretty good shock. In advance, organize your classmates and set a signal, such as raising your left hand if you sit at the front of the class, as a go-ahead. Then wait for the perfect moment. When the teacher is busily working at the board, all of you quietly slip down under your desks—and disappear!

Actually, if your teacher often tends to spend several moments at a time turned away from the the class, all of you might even be able to—very quietly of course—slip right out the door!

Note: These kinds of tricks are sometimes even more effective if two or three brave souls, out of a whole class, simply remain in their seats...acting as if nothing in any way unusual has happened.

All Together Now

You'll need:
- **class of students**

This old school trick is still a good way to break up a long day. Choose a time—say, one-thirty—and pass the word to all your classmates about what they are to do. At the agreed-upon moment—in unison—*everyone* drops their rulers, or pencils, or you all cough, or pull back your chairs, or cross your legs, or crack your knuckles, or clear your throats. To perform this trick properly, precision is critical. Everyone must perform the exact same action at the exact same time. If there's no large clock easily visible in the classroom, synchronize watches and then assign a trustworthy student at the front of the class to telegraph—and start—the action. (An electronic-age version of this trick, of course, is for the whole class to set their watch alarms for the exact same moment.)

Moving Day I

You'll need:
- **class of students**

This trick is guaranteed to disorient a teacher at least temporarily. He or she will walk into the room and sense that something is wrong but not quite be able to identify it. What the class agrees to do is to simply change seats. Even in classes where seats are not assigned, students usually choose to sit in the same places day after day, and teachers expect to see them there. When students aren't in their usual places... "What's going on?"

Moving Day II

You'll need:
- **class of students**

This moving day version requires more preparation time and is best done on a day when you know your teacher will be late. Turn everything in the classroom—your desks, the teacher's desk, any freestanding objects—90 degrees (one-quarter turn) either to the right or the left. Then sit calmly (or noisily—whatever is usual) and wait.

Sink the Sub I

You'll need:
- **substitute teacher**

There are as many ways to send a substitute teacher screaming from the room as there are kids in your class. If your teacher left a seating chart, switch seats (and thus names, too). The teacher will wonder why simply calling on a student gets big grins or a laugh.

Even without a seating chart, you can change your name. When the teacher asks, give the name of a classmate. That classmate has to pick someone else's name and so on. You can also give a different name each time you are called on. Remember, though, to stick to names of kids in the room; the teacher will most likely have a class list. You can also expand your new role by putting on an accent (French, Spanish, or Transylvanian) or a stutter.

Sink the Sub II

You'll need:
- **substitute teacher**

To do this trick, you must plan in advance and agree to it as a class. When the substitute first turns to write on the board, everyone should quietly slide their desks back about an inch. The next time, another inch; the next time, another inch—each time keeping the desks normally aligned. Without a sense of how the room usually looks, and feeling nervous and unsure in a new school, the sub probably won't really notice the small changes until it is too late: the whole class is smashed together against the back wall.

P.A. Announcement I

You'll need:
- school P.A. system
- prepared announcement

Does your school have a public address (P.A.) system? If so, it's unlikely a student can use it without a teacher finding out. But if announcements are simply read from a pile of notices, find out where it is and slip in one of your own, like: "Derek Jeter [or Brad Pitt or Britney Spears], please report to the principal's office."

P.A. Announcement II

You'll need:
- school P.A. system
- tape recorder and tape
- radio

If you can't infiltrate the school P.A. system, you'll have to fake it. At home, practice speaking in a voice that sounds like the usual P.A. announcements. Then turn on a radio and set it between stations for some authentic-sounding background static. Using a small recorder, tape a message like "Mr./Ms. X [your teacher's name], please report immediately to Mr./Ms. Y's [the principal's] office." Set the volume to the normal volume of the P.A. system. In class, hide the tape recorder until the perfect moment—just as your teacher begins to pass out a test, for example—and play your announcement.

Happy Birthday to You!

You'll need:
- **easy-going victim**

This deceptively simple trick was actually suggested by a seventh-grade math teacher. She plays it on a colleague every April Fools' Day. She walks by his classroom, peeps in, and says, "Happy Birthday, Mr. Golden!" (It's *not* his birthday.) The class bursts into cheers and singing, and much time is lost before the mistake is cleared up and her mischief is exposed. But you don't have to be a teacher to play this trick. Just be sure to choose a popular and somewhat mellow victim. Then plan to be among the last to walk into class. Before you take your seat, call out, "Happy Birthday, Mr./Ms. So-and-So!" —perhaps even present the teacher with an apple or some flowers—and enjoy the chaos and confusion that follow.

The Principal's Office

You'll need:
- **school note paper**

In some schools, kids who misbehave receive signed notes on their desks from their teacher or school principal saying, "Please see me in my office at dismissal." If you have been the sad recipient of one of these, save it. Later, make a copy —or many copies, for a stupendous effect—and drop them on the desks of your victims. Those poor souls will wonder all day which of their evil deeds has been discovered. If you do decide to create a mob in the principal's office, be sure to include yourself so that no one will suspect you.

Note: In some schools, principals also leave such notes for teachers, which suggests another version of this trick... if you dare, and if your teacher has a good sense of humor.

Invisible Ink

You'll need:
- **copy machine**

Wait until you get a long, boring worksheet for homework. Before you fill yours out, make a copy. When you get to school, sneak into your victim's homework folder. Replace the completed sheet with your blank copy. Panic time!

If you value your life, however, do *not* destroy the homework. It would be just too cruel. This is a good trick but one it is very important to be able to undo.

"Hurry, You're Late!"

You'll need:
- **brother or sister**

This is a harmless trick to play on brothers or sisters. Wake them up on a Saturday, Sunday, or holiday, crying, "Hurry, hurry! Get up! You overslept! You're gonna be late! The school bus is here!" Groggy from sleep, they'll probably believe you at least long enough to pop out of bed and whip off their pajamas. The truly gullible will not only jump up, but get dressed and rush out the door with their school bags.

School Supplies

You'll need:
- **time alone in the classroom**

Here are several good tricks for April Fools' Day, when your teacher is likely to be especially forgiving:

1) Attach all the teacher's paper clips together in one long chain.
2) Switch the tops of all the markers so that they are on pens of the wrong color.
3) Break the points of all the pencils.
4) Turn the wastebasket upside down.
5) Change the positions of the supplies.
6) Move all the desks in the classroom, turning them to face the back, or turn all the chairs around.

Crossed Eyes

You'll need:
- **eye patch**

Go to school wearing an eye patch over your left eye. Explain to your teacher and friends that you have an eye infection and will have to wear this all week. Accept their sympathy and then begin to do your work.

Midmorning, go to the bathroom and switch the patch to your right eye. At lunchtime, put it back on the left.

Midafternoon, make another switch. See how long it takes anyone to catch on. And who will it be—a teacher or one of your friends?

School Scares

You'll need:
- **an easy-going victim**

This is too mean a trick to play on someone who is the super-nervous type. But anyone who is a slacker or fairly mellow should be fair game. At about nine o'clock on a school night, call this classmate and ask whether the publication dates need to be listed in the bibliography for the (nonexistent) history paper due the next day. Or ask how his studying for the big math exam is going. Or if she was able to memorize the poem for the next day's assembly. You know best how to absolutely terrify a classmate.

4. Machine Madness

Technology is moving fast—just one step ahead of the practical jokes that make use of it. Think creatively, and you will be able to apply the basic concepts in these pranks to more advanced hardware. Parents, who tend to know less about technology than kids, make the best targets.

Wake-up Call

You'll need:
- **alarm clock or clock radio**

Almost every grown-up's bedroom these days has an alarm clock—the perfect prop for a practical joke. You can bring your victim back from dreamland to one of several rude surprises. The simplest trick is simply to set the alarm an hour earlier than usual. Or, on Saturday or Sunday, turn it on to the regular weekday wake-up time. Or, don't change it at all; just hide it!

With a clock radio, you have additional options. You can change the station—from one that plays soothing classical music, for example, to a station that plays heavy metal. Arrange for an added jolt by turning the volume up several notches. For a triple whammy, try three of these alarming tricks at once. But keep in mind that grown-ups' sense of humor can be very, very thin in the morning, especially if they haven't had a full night's restful sleep.

False Alarm

You'll need:
- **tape recorder and tape**

Monday morning is a particularly cruel time to play this trick. Make a tape of 30 seconds of silence followed by the alarm ringing for 5 minutes. To do this, first set the alarm and let it run its natural course. Then start it over as often as necessary, rewinding the tape a bit each time so that there is no pause between rings. (You may want to leave the room during the taping sessions.)

Note the time for which the clock alarm is set on Sunday night. Just before that time the next morning, sneak into the room. Turn off the alarm and hide your tape recorder with its 5-minute alarm tape in an unlikely spot. Press the "Play" button and slip silently out. You may want to watch from outside the door as your half-asleep victim tries hopelessly to douse the sound.

Time Flies

You'll need:
- **clock or alarm clock**

To play this trick, simply move the clock ahead by one hour. Wake up early in the morning and sneak into your brother's, or sister's, or parents' bedroom. Turn off the clock alarm if it is set. Then move the small hand one hour forward. Your victims will probably wake up when they usually do even without the alarm. They will look at the clock, assume that they turned off the alarm in their sleep—and panic. Sure that they are late for work or school, they will switch immediately into high gear, racing around madly. Watch out, though, when they figure out what happened—and who did it! A slightly milder version of this trick is to move the clock ahead late in the afternoon when your parents are expecting dinner guests.

If you can reach the clock in your classroom and your teacher is a good egg, try this trick at school. But remember, the new dismissal time on the clock should match the school's schedule of bells.

Weight Watchers

You'll need:
- **bathroom scale**

It seems everyone is worried about gaining weight. There are scales in every home and even in some hotel bathrooms. There are even tiny traveling scales so weight watchers can take them on trips. Traditional spring scales are usually easy to adjust. For an effective trick, turn the tiny knob that sets the starting weight to something higher than zero. If you push it ahead just a few pounds—2 or 3—your victim will likely be merely depressed at having "gained." More than that at a time and he or she will become suspicious.

Electronic scales are harder to tamper with: they are set at the factory. But some can be switched to kilograms—for a ridiculously low reading when someone thinks they are reading pounds (there are about 2.2 pounds to a kilogram).

Lights Out

You'll need:
  • **lamp**

Some of the simplest tricks are the best—and what could be simpler than unplugging a lamp? (Remember: pull the plug, not the cord.) This trick is most effective, of course, if the plug is hidden—behind a bed or couch, for example.

Another simple trick is to loosen a light bulb by turning it counterclockwise in the socket (touch only the bulb and handle it carefully) just far enough to lose the electrical contact but not so much that it falls out. If you "fix" all the lights in a room by just loosening them, your victims will suspect a short circuit and probably fuss with the fuse box for quite awhile before discovering the trick. If you do just one lamp, they'll simply suspect that the bulb has burned out and go to get a new one to put in. (In that case, for an added twist why not hide the supply of light bulbs?) The best site for the one-bulb version is the reading light many grown-ups have beside or above their beds.

Actually, the trick of unplugging works not just lamps. You can apply the same mischief to almost anything that requires electricity: kitchen appliances, radios, or televisions. If a plug is hidden so your victim can't see that it's loose, but you can reach it, there's a trick.

If a wall switch controls some lamps in your house, what would happen if you carefully move a small appliance or two, plug them into those lamp sockets, and turn them on? When the wall switch is flicked on, instead of the expected "light," your victim will be startled by the blender roaring to life or the radio blasting in the darkness.

Bells Are Ringing

You'll need:
- **tape recorder and tape**

Do you remember ever watching a TV show where the phone on the screen rang and you thought it was your own? If you have a tape recorder, you can turn this illusion into a practical joke.

Notice when your telephone is usually answered (after the second, third, or fourth ring). Make a tape of 30 seconds of silence and then the phone ringing one time less than the usual pickup. Then tape 5 minutes of silence. Repeat this until you have three sets of rings followed by silence. Then tape 10 rings. Play back the tape and adjust the volume to match that of the real ring. Rewind the tape. Hide the tape recorder near the telephone and turn it on. The perfect victim will run to answer the telephone three times, growing angrier at the rude caller who keeps hanging up. Not until the fourth time—with the long ring—will it become obvious that this is a trick.

Sound FX

You'll need:
- **tape recorder and tape**

Certain sounds drive people crazy: squeaky floors and drippy faucets, for example. Other sounds can be mysterious or bewildering: a cat meowing or a dog barking in a petless household, birds chirping in the wintertime, rain pattering on the roof or air conditioner on a sunny day, or a baby crying where there is no baby. For this trick, use your tape recorder to capture five or ten minutes of annoying or out of place sounds. Precede it with ten minutes of silence on the tape. This will give you time to set up the recorder and leave the area—so that you can look as totally innocent and baffled as everyone else. Be sure to hide the tape recorder where it will be clearly heard, but where your parents or siblings are unlikely to look.

Talking to Yourself

You'll need:
- **tape recorder and tape**

This is a prank for budding playwrights. Write a dialogue between two characters, both of them you. One of you should be talking to the other from a different room. Tape one character's lines, starting with, "Hey, Cindy [or Mike, or Noodles, or whatever your name is]!" and leaving about five seconds blank for a response. (You may need longer, depending on your script.) Leave about a minute blank at the start of the tape so that you have time to leave the room after you turn it on and go nearby where there are other people (your audience). Once the tape starts playing, calling out to you, your conversation with yourself begins.

Help!

You'll need:
  • **walkie-talkie**

Put one walkie-talkie, with the volume turned up high, on the top shelf of a cold oven. Leave the oven door slightly ajar. When you see someone approaching the kitchen, speak loudly into the other walkie-talkie: "Hey! Is anybody out there?" "Help, please! I'm stuck!" "I need help! It's hot in here." "Pleeease, help! I'm sooo hot!" Each time, speak more urgently, but wait a few seconds between cries so your victim will have trouble tracking the sound. Don't forget to "rescue" the walkie-talkie from the oven after the laughs.

Computer Virus

You'll need:
- **computer**

Do *not* attempt this trick unless you are a computer whiz. If you fail to undo it at the end, your victims will probably undo you.

The exact details to inciting panic depends on the kind of computer you are using, but the trick is to hide your victim's work without losing it. There's nothing more upsetting than to turn on your computer to finish your homework, your novel, your taxes, or even your grocery list, and find that it's vanished. Adults, especially, tend to be terrified of such computer antics and may conclude in despair and without investigating further that the foul machine has simply gobbled up their words: "It's gone!"

On some computers, you can hide documents by moving them from one file folder to another. On some, all you have to do is rename the document. As easy as all this may seem, the key to having fun with this kind of prank is: If in doubt of your abilities, don't do it!

One final safeguard: It's a good idea to print anything out before "messing" with it. Then, if you should make a mistake and actually lose something, you'll at least have the hard copy to deliver with your apology and an offer to type it in again.

5. Phony Phone Calls

All that these jokes require is a bit of dramatic flair. Unfortunately, new phone technology may spoil your fun, if your victim can see who is calling. One option is to disable this service when you place your call. Some carriers may do it for free; others charge a fee. Be sure to find out before racking up unknown costs—or the joke might turn out to be on you. Of course, you *could* just make the calls (local, of course)…and take your chances.

Phone-y Messages

You'll need:
- **telephone**

Next time one of your parents or your brother or sister is out, or you are baby-sitting for a very good-natured family, leave one of these phony telephone messages with the appropriate return number:

Mr. Lyons (or Mr. Wolfe) called (phone number for the zoo)
Ms. Reed called (the library)
Mr. Cooke called (a fancy restaurant)
Mrs. Rich called (a bank)
Mr. Rhodes called (the American Automobile Association)
Ms. Katz called (a veterinarian)
Ms. Sweet called (a bakery)
Mr. Burger called (a butcher)
Ms. Chips called (a computer store)
Mr. Roach called (an exterminator)
Ms. Wood called (a lumberyard)
Mr. Diamond called (a jeweler)
Mrs. Green called (a plant store)

Now think up some of your own.

Phone Phooler

You'll need:
- **telephone**

Choose a name and address randomly from the telephone book, or choose a friend or an acquaintance to call, if you are able to disguise your voice well. Phone your victim and ask things such as the following:

"Do you live on [name of his or her street]?"
The answer will be "Yes."
"Then you'd better get out of the way; a car is coming."

"Does [name of street] run by your house?"
Again, "Yes."
"Then go out and catch it."

"Is your refrigerator running?"
"Yes."
"You'd better hurry and catch it."

If your victim is willing to talk, it's possible to prolong the fun:

You: "May I speak to Robert Wall, please."
Victim: "You must have the wrong number. There is no Robert Wall here."
Y: "Is there a Susan Wall?"
V: "No."
Y: "What about Peter Wall?"
V: "No."
Y: "Stephanie Wall?"
V: "No."
Y: "You mean there are no Walls in your house?"

V: "No, there aren't."

Y: "Then what holds up your ceiling?"

The nice thing about this sort of practical joke is that your phone phooler fun is only limited by your imagination and creativity.

Conference Calls

You'll need:
- **telephone with "conference call" feature**

Many telephones these days have a "Conference Call" or "Three-Way Calling" feature which can be used to make all sorts of mismatches. Connect a Chinese restaurant with a French restaurant; a veterinarian with a beauty salon; a waterproofing contractor with an aquarium, a pet store with a zoo; two people who don't know each other; or two people who do. Although telephone systems work differently (you will have to learn your own), the basic trick is to place the first call and say, "Will you hold one moment, please?" Then quickly place the second call. Just as that person picks up, start the conference. You will have the pleasure of listening in on the chaos you have caused.

Body Parts

You'll need:
- **telephone**

These are wise-guy jokes. Call the butcher and ask, "Do you have pigs' feet?" "Yes." "How do you get your shoes on?" Or "Do you have chicken [or frogs'] legs?... Where do you find pants to fit?"

Call the grocer and ask, "Do you have a tongue?" (Pick a store where you expect to get "No" for an answer.) "Then how can you be talking on the phone?" Or "Do you have brains?" (Again, call someone you expect will say "No.") "Then how do you keep your books?"

Call the baker and ask, "Do you have elephant ears?... You must look awfully strange." Or, if the baker is a man, "Do you have ladyfingers?... I guess you must shop for gloves in the women's department."

Let Him Out!

You'll need:
- **telephone**

The original butt of this joke was the tobacconist, at a time when pipe-smoking was more common than it is today. Ask your grandfather if he ever called up a tobacco store when he was a kid and asked, "Do you have Prince Albert [a brand of tobacco] in the can?" "Yes" would be the innocent reply. "Then let him out!"

You may not know of a tobacconist, but try this joke on a tea shop or the tea section of a gourmet store: "Do you have Prince Edward in a tin [or in bags]?" Or at a supermarket: "Do you have Rosemary [or Basil or Ginger] in a jar?" or "Do you have Olive Oil in a can?" (The answer to this last one is, "This is Popeye speaking; you'd better let her out.")

Leave Your Message After the Beep

You'll need:
- **telephone answering machine**

To do answering machine tricks, you need to disguise your voice. Practice speaking with a very high or low voice. If neither works, recruit a helper who can sound grown-up. Then call your own telephone number when no one is home and leave a mysterious or bizarre message. You may pretend to be the school principal, calling your parents to report that their child (you) has gone wild and swallowed all the newts in the science room. Or you could be a lawyer, leaving the message that your father has inherited a fortune from a long lost third cousin he never knew. To make the joke more elaborate, use the name of a real law firm (look in the Yellow Pages under "Lawyers"), use a last name from the firm's name (e.g., Sidney Glork of Blork, Glork, and Dork), and leave the firm's real telephone number. Or, simply pick a name and telephone number from the phone book and leave the message to please call back.

Home Secretary

You'll need:
- **telephone**
- **accomplices**

Unless you are extraordinarily clever at disguising your voice, you will need several accomplices for this joke. First, have one of your accomplices call the victim on the telephone and ask, "May I speak to Sidney Plunkett [or some other made-up name], please?" When told, "You have the wrong number," the caller should apologize politely and hang up. At about 10-minute intervals, have two or three more accomplices make the same call, asking for the same name. Then, after another 10 minutes, you (or the last caller) should dial. When the victim picks up this time, you say, "Hello, this is Sidney Plunkett. Did I get any messages?"

You've Reached...

You'll need:
• **telephone**

You can play some quick tricks at your end of the line, too. When the telephone rings at your house, get to the phone first and answer, "Hello. City Morgue. Can we help you?" Or "Overeaters Anonymous," "Santa's Workshop," "Psychic Research," "Ghostbusters," "Matchmaking Service," or any other weird response you can come up with.

Rrrringgg!

You'll need:
• **telephone**
• **clear tape**

A simple, extremely frustrating trick is to stick down, using clear tape, one of the buttons in the cradle of your telephone. Then, when someone picks up the phone, it will continue to ring or there won't be a dial tone. For awhile at least, he or she will be mystified, and will push every button in sight.

Utilities

You'll need:
- **telephone**

For these tricks to work, you will need to disguise your voice and sound like an adult, or find a friend who can. In the early evening, phone your home from a friend's house:

1. Explain that you work for the telephone company and that for the next hour you will be cleaning the phone lines. Ask your mother or father to lay the phone on a cloth, which can catch the dust or dirt that will be blown through the line.

2. Explain that you are from the telephone company and that service people will be working on the lines for the next two hours. If the telephone rings, under no circumstances should anyone answer it, as this could result in electrocuting one of the workers. Then call about every ten minutes. After a while even the best intentioned grown-up will give in or forget. When the phone is answered, scream in agony into the receiver.

3. Explain that you are from the city plumbing department. You will be shutting off the water in the pipes for service until noon the next day. You are notifying all residents in the area so that they can fill their tubs and pots with water and avoid flushing the toilet.

6. Midnight Mischief

Night is the ideal time for ghosts and ghouls…and pranksters. Victims are at their most vulnerable—available and unaware. The most important and the hardest part of all these tricks is simply keeping quiet while you do your evil. No giggling or cackling!

Short Sheets

You'll need:
- **bed made with 2 sheets**

Short-sheeting a bed is a popular trick at camp and in college dormitories. Try this at home, instead, where no one will be expecting it. Here is how to short-sheet a bed: First, tuck the bottom sheet all the way around, as you normally do. The tricky part is next: making the top sheet look like both the top and bottom sheets. First spread out the sheet and tuck it in at the top of the bed. Fold the sheet bottom to come to about 12 inches from the top, or however you ordinarily arrange the top sheet. Tuck in the sides as usual. When your victim crawls wearily into bed, eager to stretch out and relax, he or she will be trapped at the fold.

Strange Bedfellows

You'll need:
- **made bed**
- **corn flakes, rubber snake, etc.**

This is an old favorite with many possible variations. All you have to do is use your imagination. Your victim climbs into bed and stretches out, ready to go to sleep and…what's that?

There are plenty of bedtime surprises to spring. A layer of potato chips or crunchy cereal under the bottom sheet will add snap and crackle…if you don't mind the cleanup afterward. Or how about some peas or beans: Do you remember "The Princess and the Pea" story? A stiff hairbrush, a rubber snake, or some tickly fake insect stuffed under the top sheet, about three-quarters of the way down, will be an unwelcome surprise. For an extra shock, put these "attackers" in the freezer for an hour or two; then tuck them between the sheets just before bedtime.

Pie in the Face

You'll need:
- **shaving or whipped cream**
- **feather or piece of yarn**

This is known as a staple at sleepover parties, so even if you decide not to do it on someone else, beware—someone may try it on you! You will need a can of shaving cream or, if you are kinder, whipped cream. More important, though, is to choose the right sort of victim: someone with an excellent sense of humor and a forgiving heart. Wait until this poor good-natured soul is sound asleep, ideally face-up and with a favored hand lying free. As quietly as possible, spray some cream into the victim's open hand. Then tickle his or her nose with a feather, piece of yarn, or thread. This will create an irresistible urge to scratch—with what shocking and messy results you can well imagine.

Interior Redecoration

You'll need:
- **a very sound sleeper**

College students have been known to play this trick on zonked out roommates, but it can also work on a brother, sister, mother, father, or friend. In the college version, after waiting until the victim is sound asleep, students completely strip the bedroom, leaving the bed and sleeper stranded in a bare space. Slightly less strenuous, but also requiring help, is to turn a victim's twin-size bed completely around with him or her in it, so that the view in the morning is totally reversed.

For a less stunning effect, you might empty dresser drawers, switch their order around, clear off any or all flat surfaces, and remove all framed pictures from the walls. Moving small pieces of furniture, lamps, or toys to new spots can cause morning confusion, too.

Sleeping Beauty

You'll need:
 • **face paints**

For this trick, which can be done at home or on a sleepover, choose a victim who is a sound sleeper, ideally one who sleeps face up. Sneak into the bedroom early in the morning with a set of face paints…and create.

You may choose to paint a realistic blemish or wound— a mole, a garden of freckles, a bloody nose, a big red pimple, or a black eye. Make your artwork large and visible to catch your victim's eye in the bathroom mirror before it is washed away. Another possibility is a complete transformation: turn your victim into a cat, a dog, a devil, a werewolf, or a clown.

And the face need not be your only canvas. Any exposed body parts are fair game, so long as the face paints used are washable and don't stain (check the packaging!). Imagine your big brother getting out a sock and noticing his big toe turned into the head of a green snake…or a little gray mouse.

Polish Him Off

You'll need:
- **nail polish**

This is a good trick for a male relative or friend. In preparation, borrow or buy a bottle of brightly colored nail polish. Hide any polish remover you have in the house. One weeknight, sneak into your victim's room when he is sleeping soundly. Paint as many of his fingernails as you can reach. Then try to get out of the house early the next morning before he wakes up.

Going Gray Overnight

You'll need:
- **baby powder**

Maybe your parents have said, "The things you do—you are making me gray before my time." Well, now you can do it up right, and overnight. And the only equipment you need is a container of baby powder. The hard part of this trick will be staying awake until your parents are both sound asleep. That's when you sneak into the bedroom, shake some powder onto your hand and gently pat or drop it onto your victims' hair. If you do it to both parents, they will look in the mirror in the morning—or at each other—and be shocked. Be very careful and gentle, though. If you rub the powder in too hard or get it on or too near their faces and they wake up—you could be the one in danger of getting gray hair.

7. Body Basics

These tricks, more than any others, require keeping a poker face. If you can't tell a simple fib without cracking a smile, you might want to take a pass on them. On the other hand, here's your chance for an award-winning performance, or at least a very satisfactory wild audience reaction.

Cold Feet

You'll need:
- **ice cube**
- **plastic bag with twist tie**

Here's a first-thing-in-the-morning trick, well worth waking up early for. Put an ice cube in a small plastic bag and seal or twist-tie it tightly (double bag, if needed). Then slip this frozen delight deep into one of your victim's shoes. Try to be nearby to enjoy the moment of contact. And don't limit your mischief to shoes. You can also drop ice-cube bags into boots, slippers, mittens, coat pockets, knitted hats, and kitchen mitts.

Earrings and Nose Rings

You'll need:
- **beads and glue, or**
- **clip-on jewelry**

Have you been just too good lately? Do you want to give your parents a shock? Come home one day from school, or a sleep-over, and announce that you have had your ears or your nose pierced. And, you'll be wearing the jewelry to prove it.

There are two ways to create this illusion. You can buy clip-on hoops for your ears and nose that look exactly like the pierced ones. Or you can use a spot of white glue to attach fake jewels or small glass, metal, or plastic beads to your nose or your ears. Hold them in place for a few minutes until the glue dries, for a "makeover" that's easily undoable.

Put Up Your Dukes

You'll need:
- **an accomplice**

There is nothing that upsets grown-ups more than seeing kids fight. You can give them a real scare with some of the tricks that actors use to stage fights for plays and movies.

1. K.O.: Kid A throws a fake punch at Kid B's face or stomach. She stops short, but slaps her side with her free hand to make the sound of a hit. Kid B falls back as if struck. (Tip: Make sure the audience is on the side of Kid A's punching hand.)

2. Face Slap: With her left hand on Kid B's right cheek, Kid A pretends to slap Kid B with her right hand. Actually she moves her left hand away and slaps that instead. (Tip: The audience should be on Kid B's left side.)

3. Ear Lift: Kid A (the bigger one) covers Kid B's ears with his hands, but does not grab hold of them. Kid B grasps Kid A's forearms. Kid A lifts Kid B with his arms and Kid B thrashes his legs as if trying to escape. It will look as if Kid B is being lifted by the ears.

4. Caveman Hair-Pull: Kid A kneels on the floor. Kid B puts a hand on Kid A's head as if grabbing his hair. Kid B puts his hands on top of Kid A's and rocks back and forth vigorously, as if Kid A is yanking him around.

5. Banging Your Head Against the Wall: This is a trick you can do alone. Walk up to a wall. Start to bang your head but stop before making contact. At just the moment your head would have hit, kick the wall hard with your foot. Do this over and over.

With practice and sound effects (groans, moans, cries and grunts), these staged tricks will horrify any grown-ups around.

Severed Finger

You'll need:
- **small cardboard box**
- **red food coloring or ketchup**

This trick is not for the weak of heart or stomach. Find a small cardboard box, the kind that sometimes holds jewelry. Poke a hole near one end of the bottom wide enough to fit your right index finger through. Insert your finger, holding the bottom of the box with your middle finger and your thumb. Meanwhile stretch your index finger out onto the bottom of the box. You can dress up the box with cotton and dress up the base of the finger with "blood" (red food coloring or ketchup). Set the top back on the box and approach your victim. "Look what I found!" you might say, though feel free to improvise. Then open the box with your left hand. To complete the effect, start to wiggle the finger a bit.

A Bloody Mess

You'll need:
- **corn syrup**
- **red and yellow food colorings**

Fake blood can be used for a vast number of tricks to fool and frighten grown-ups, especially parents. Just be sure to "recover" from your wounds quickly, before anyone panics or faints, or calls 911 or an ambulance.

The basic storyline for this trick is a loud crash followed

by a scream. Then a child (you) rushes in, seemingly crying and covered with blood. The crash sound can be noise from a snare drum, if you have one. If not, overturn a mountain of wooden blocks or anything else unbreakable.

To make the blood, start with half a cup of corn syrup. Add five drops of red food coloring to one drop of yellow. For a deeper color, continue to add the food colorings in the same proportions. (Test the color on your skin.) If needed, thin the mixture by adding a little water.

Face Lift

You'll need:
- **clown or other makeup**

First, to prepare, cover the bottom of a small plate with a very thin coating of various makeup (clown white, blush, eye shadow, other) so that it isn't easily noticeable. Tell your victim that you have learned hypnosis. Would he like to be your first subject? "Why not?" he'll answer. Tell him to look directly into your eyes and do exactly as you say and do.

Come close to him and, gazing into his eyes, hand him the plate, holding it low. "Here, take this plate and rub your finger around the bottom," you say in a soothing, hypnotic voice. "Now, bring your finger up to your face [mimic the motions with your own finger], and around and around your eyes. Now around your nose"…and so on. If the makeup runs out, have him return his finger to the bottom of the plate.

Finally, ask if he is now under your spell. He will say "No," and you can say, "Thanks, anyway. I must need more practice" while you whisk the telltale plate away.

Ah-choo!

You'll need:
- **glass of water**

This trick does not appeal to all jokers. It is actually a little bit disgusting.

Have a full glass of water in hand near you on a table. Then wait for your victim. You need to be in position behind this person's back.

Once you have your victim in place, the stage is set. Put two fingers into the glass of water and give an elephant-like sneeze as you flick the water from your fingers onto the back of your victim's neck. Yuck!

Sticky Feet

You'll need:
- **wall**
- **doorway**

Here are three tricks to fool your brothers, sisters, and friends about what their bodies can and can't do.

1. Foot Lift: Ask your victims to stand against a wall. Their right cheek, arm, and foot should be pressing against the wall. Then ask them to lift their left foot. "No problem," they will say. But, oops! It's stuck to the floor. Why? They can't shift their weight off that foot because the wall prevents them from leaning farther to the right.

2. Tiptoes: Have your victims stand against the edge of an open door so that their nose and stomach touch it and their feet are straddling it. Ask them to go up on their tiptoes. They can't. This time, they need to shift their weight forward and the door is in the way.

3. Hip-Hop: Ask your victims to grab onto the toe ends of their shoes with both hands. Now ask them to hop forward. No go. They can't lean over far enough to hop; they will topple over first.

8. Expect the Unexpected

Here are a wide variety of jokes—indoor and outdoor, long and short, old and new, simple and complex—all of which make a big splash. Save them for a special person on a special day. Then find a safe place to hide.

Bathroom Booby Traps

You'll need:
- **petroleum jelly, or**
- **roll of toilet paper and glue**

The bathroom is the perfect setting for practical jokes. Your victim is already trapped in what could be an embarrassing position behind a closed door. The classic bathroom joke is to spread a thin layer of petroleum jelly over the toilet seat. For an added touch, spread some on the inside doorknob, too.

Toilet paper is another excellent instrument of torture. Many people become distressed even if the roll is inserted so they have to pull from the front rather than the back—or vice versa, whichever they are not used to. And most everyone becomes hysterical at finding no toilet paper at all!

Just removing the toilet paper roll, however, is too easy —a beginner's joke. Instead, choose an ample-looking toilet paper roll. Run a glue stick or a thin line of white glue along the open edge of the outermost sheet and press it against the roll. When it dries, install it in the bathroom. Your victim, expecting to catch hold of the loose end, will turn the roll one way and the other, more and more frantically each time.

Shaving-Cream Willies

You'll need:
- **shaving cream**

Here is a use for shaving cream that the manufacturer never imagined. It's also a practical joke with good shock value for little effort and minimal damage. Simply smear some shaving cream on a toilet seat. This is best done in your own home. If you do it while visiting, your victim should be someone you either know very well or never want to see again. You'll need a white surface, not designer color, so the coating is not immediately visible.

Trick-or-Treat

You'll need:
- Halloween costume
- co-conspirators

Here is a way to put more fright, and fun, into Halloween, that colorful holiday celebrated on October 31. On the day before, on October 30, gather a group of friends, dress up in costumes, and start knocking on doors. Under your masks, you will be able to fully enjoy the flustered gasps and shrieks of neighbors, afraid that they've mistaken the date and imagining a long night of ringing doorbells, with nothing to offer those relentless hoards of ghosts, witches, and superheroes. Be sure to keep your mask on during the prank and change costumes for the official night, so you won't be denied treats when you ring again.

Secret Admirer

You'll need:
- **Valentine's Day card and postage**
- **telephone book**

Did you ever receive a Valentine signed, "from your Secret Admirer"? It's usually pretty easy to figure out who that is. But what if you can't—drives you crazy, right? Well, next Valentine's Day, pick a name out of the telephone book and send him or her a card signed, "from your Secret Admirer." Unlike most practical jokes, you won't have the satisfaction of seeing your victim's surprise; but just imagining it will probably give you a lot of chuckles.

Do Unto Others

You'll need:
- **coins**
- **car trip toll**

Here's another puzzle-a-stranger trick to use during a boring car trip. When you stop to pay a toll (a small one—no more than a dollar), give the driver an extra payment to pass to the attendant saying, "We're also paying for the car behind."

You might be able to get a glimpse of the confusion in the rear view mirror as you drive away. Even if you don't, you'll chuckle every time you think of those riders in the car behind, who will probably spend the rest of the day wondering who you are and why you paid the toll for them.

Sleeveless Errand

You'll need:
- **gullible victim**

The "sleeveless" errand (aka "wild-goose chase") is a standard joke played on April Fools' Day in England. It probably will work best for you with a younger brother or sister. Tell your victim that you are working on a project for school and need some help. Could he or she please run out to the store or ask a grown-up for something important that you are missing? (The item you need for your non-existent project is something that sounds real but actually couldn't possibly exist.)

Here are some suggestions for sleeveless errand items: elbow grease, black whitewash, a left-handed monkey wrench, the key to a pitcher's box, the key to an oarlock, a bucket of steam, a bottle stretcher, six bumblebee feathers, a 4-foot yardstick, a dozen buttonholes, a pint of pigeon's milk, smooth sandpaper, a bottle of dotted ink, a can of striped paint. Get the idea? Now use your imagination to come up with some special "needs" of your own.

Wrap It Up

You'll need:
- **4 to 6 gift boxes of different sizes**
- **tissue paper, wrapping paper, bow**

For this trick, you will need to prepare secretly in advance. Save tissue paper and gift boxes of different sizes from birthday parties and holiday presents. Then wait for a time when you want to give a gift. Write "Happy Birthday!," "Surprise!," "April Fool!," or whatever greeting you wish on a card. Then wrap it over and over and over again in tissue paper. Put this in the smallest box. Wrap it over and over and over in tissue paper and put this in the next box. Again, wrap it…. Repeat this process until you have filled your largest box. The more boxes the better. Cover the last box in wrapping paper, tie it with a bow, and deliver it with a smile.

The Waiting Game

You'll need:
- **a long string**

Are you a good actor? If so, then get a very long piece of string and try this trick. Find a kind, gullible-looking victim waiting on the street or at a bus stop. Tell him that you have a measuring project to do for school which will take only a minute. Ask him to hold one end of the string while you run around the corner. You will be right back. Once you turn the corner, look for your next victim. Tell him the same story, hand him the end of the string, and run forward as if you are returning to the source of the string. If you fail to find a second victim, the joke will still work nicely. Simply tie the string to a lamp post or tree and wait in hiding to see how long it stays taut.

Hunting the Gawk

You'll need:
   • note paper

A gawk is a cuckoo bird, and gawk hunting is a special Scottish April Fools' joke. The victim is given a sealed letter and told to deliver it to Person A. The letter reads, "This is the first of April. Hunt the gawk another mile." Person A reseals the letter and tells the victim to deliver it to Person B. Person B does the same, and on and on until finally the victim catches on. Try a version of this trick on your younger brother or sister. Your note might say: "This is an April Fools' joke. Tell [the victim] that this message is not for you. Give him [or her] directions to deliver it to someone else."

Catch Me Quick!

You'll need:
- **clear nylon thread**

This neat trick can be played on an adult without too much danger of upset, just a little gasp of surprise.

Choose a small item belonging to your victim—keys, wallet, notebook. Then, when he or she is out of the room, attach a long piece of clear nylon thread to the object and place it on the floor or ground in plain sight. Sit nearby holding the other end of the thread taut in your hand, as low to the ground as possible. As the owner returns, spots the item, and reaches for it, pull the string to slide the item away. And the chase is on!

Rock and Roll

You'll need:
- **medium-sized rock**
- **paint and paintbrush**

There is said to be a rock planted by jokers on a trail in Georgia with these words painted on the top: TURN ME OVER. On the other side are these words: NOW TURN ME BACK SO THAT I MAY FOOL ANOTHER.

You don't have to wait until you are in Georgia to enjoy this trick. Paint a rock of your own and plant it in a neighbor's backyard, behind the school, or in the woods where your friends are likely to see it.

R-r-r-r-i-p

You'll need:
- **sheet of typing paper**

Make a little starter tear in the middle of the shorter side of a sheet of typing paper and hold it behind your back. Choose a victim who is wearing a tight skirt or fitted pants. You can either wait patiently until he or she bends over naturally or say you are doing a physical fitness survey on how many people can touch their toes. Then, when your unsuspecting victim has reached about halfway down, tear the paper the rest of the way. Guess what it sounds like! Adults (a parent or even a teacher) are the best victims for this kind of practical joke; they tend to embarrass easily.

Found Money

You'll need:
- **shiny coin (a penny won't do)**
- **chewing gum or a strong glue**

Did you ever walk along and suddenly spot a coin on the ground in front of you? You probably looked around for someone who might have dropped it and, if no one was in sight, scooped it up happily. What if the coin refused to be scooped, but stuck to the ground? Put a glob of well-chewed gum or quick-stick glue on the back of a quarter or other coin. With your foot, press it onto a flat sidewalk, boardwalk, or playground. Then step aside and wait for a victim.

The Sky Is Falling

You'll need:
- **shoebox and packing, pillow, or water balloon**

This is an old trick, modified for indoor use and safety. In its classic form, a bucket of water is rigged to the top of a door so that, when the door is pushed open, its contents fall on the victim's head. For our version, rig a shoebox full of packing peanuts, or a pillow, or a knotted water-filled balloon (the water balloon is probably better saved for your cabin door at camp). Open the door just far enough to rest your "bomb" on top, tipping slightly toward the outside of the door (practice the placement beforehand). As your victim pushes the door open to enter, the "sky" starts falling down.

April (Fools' Day) Showers

You'll need:
- **collapsible umbrella**
- **powder, flour, or cornmeal**

Many umbrellas booby-trap themselves—by refusing to open or stay open, or by turning themselves inside-out in the wind. But you can also give the family umbrella a helping hand. All you need is a collapsible umbrella, with at least one bend in its ribs, and about one-quarter cup of flour, powder, or cornmeal. Open the umbrella and lay it upside down on the ground. Pour the flour into the middle, spreading it as far out as the bends in the ribs. Carefully close up the umbrella and hook the outside strap tightly. When your victim opens the umbrella, the flour will come showering down. (If it happens indoors, that's double bad luck!)

Water Torture

You'll need:
- **glass of water**

Fill a glass with water, then play it cool. Don't tell your victim that you are about to do a trick. Just say something like, "Watch this. Lay your two index fingers together at the edge of the table, pointing toward the far edge [you might have to demonstrate]." As soon as he or she puts those fingers down, quickly balance the glass of water on them. By the time your victim has figured out what has happened, it will be too late. There's no way out except to spill the water.

Wishbone

You'll need:
- **a prearranged phone call**

This trick, from Yugoslavia, got its name because it starts with two people holding opposite sides of a chicken wishbone and making a bet. One bets that he can get the other to accept something unknowingly. Here, you don't need a wishbone to make that bet. Before you do, though, arrange for a friend to call you on the phone. When it rings, pick it up and say, "Hello." Listen for a few seconds, then say, "Hold on, please." Hand it to your victim, with the words, "It's for you." If he takes the phone, you win the bet.

Rubber-necking

You'll need:
- **gullible strangers**

Get a group of friends to help you with this one. Stand on the sidewalk together, all looking up at a tall building or into a tree, as if something extraordinary is perched there. Very likely, pretty soon others will gather around to look too. If anyone asks a question, say, "Shhh…," as if the object of your gaze might be scared away. Once the crowd is big enough, turn to the person next to you and ask what everyone is looking at.

All Washed Up

You'll need:
- **a sink with a spray nozzle**
- **clear tape**

Some sinks have a special hose with a spray nozzle that sits next to the faucet. If you are lucky enough to have one of these, you have a practical joke made-to-order. Turn the nozzle to face the front of the sink. Then tape down the lever that opens the water flow, so that it is ready to go when the faucet is turned on. Now you just need to hope that you are in the kitchen to see "spray time" in action.

Designer Labels

You'll need:
- **t-shirts**

Certain designers splash their names and logos all over their clothes. Others limit their advertising to a subtle label just inside the back of the shirt neck. Those are the ones you need. Some summer night go into the drawers of your parents and siblings and turn their t-shirts inside out. Be sure to pick plain colors (reversed designs are too easy to spot), and fold them back neatly where they were. Although you're unlikely to be present at the moment of discovery, you can be sure your victim will be thoroughly embarrassed when finally told "Your t-shirt is inside out."

Psychological Warfare

You'll need:
- **gullible victim**

This is the ultimate April Fools' Day joke. You will need no props and no preparation; just some first-class acting. It begins the night before. "You know what tomorrow is, don't you?" you say. "April Fools' Day. And do I have terrific tricks planned! I can't wait." Then rub your hands together gleefully. The next day keep hinting that something really big is about to happen. Your victims will worry all day long and into the night. They will even be afraid to go to bed. The joke, of course, is that you are bluffing. You have no jokes planned at all.

Index